PRAISES FOR
DIARY OF EMOTIONS

"While the entire Finding Mother Series provides a window into dealing with a loved one who suffers from a mental illness, this final book, *Diary of Emotions*, speaks to the heart of the struggle the author has gone through. Her in-depth, conflicting emotions covered throughout this book offer a raw and real view of the complexities of love and acceptance." **~Leslie Arambula, MA in Creative Writing, English Teacher**

"I like the vulnerability shown in *Diary of Emotions*. The author captured the true essence of being enthralled in emotions as she stepped outside of her own understanding to gain new awareness and insight into her mother's mental illness. This book could benefit secondary school students." **~Jacob Kelow, M.S.Ed., Secondary School Counselor, Kansas City Public Schools**

"I thoroughly enjoyed every book in the *Finding Mother Series*, but *Diary of Emotions* was my favorite." **~Dimitra Manda, BA in English Language and Literature, English Teacher**

"In *Diary of Emotions*, the author openly shares her desires, experiences, and uncertainties after reuniting with her mother." **~Dr. Mary E. McConnell, Educator, University of Missouri – Kansas City**

"When someone in your family has a mental illness, it is easy to say, 'I am going to look past their behavior because I understand that they have a mental illness.'

"Nevertheless, that does not take away the pain that comes with not having the type of relationship that you would like to have with them.

"Sometimes, I wonder what is harder: living without a mother and not knowing her, or knowing her and having to live with the reality of her mental illness."

~**Grace LaJoy Henderson**
Diary of Emotions, Page 70

Dr. Grace LaJoy Henderson

DIARY

OF

EMOTIONS

Thoughts and Feelings

Inspirations by Grace LaJoy
Raymore, MO 64083

DIARY OF EMOTIONS: THOUGHTS AND FEELINGS
Grace LaJoy Henderson

Disclaimer. I have tried to recreate events, locales and conversations from my memories of them. In order to maintain their anonymity in some instances I have changed the names of individuals and places. I may have changed some identifying characteristics and details such as physical properties, occupations and places of residence.

Due to the delicate subject of mental illness, all names are fictitious. I have taken great precaution to ensure my mother could not be located, while still sharing my real-life story.

Mission. Sharing my story to help increase awareness of mental illness.

Goal. Reducing stigma. Fostering connection. Inspiring hope.

DIARY OF EMOTIONS: THOUGHTS AND FEELINGS
Copyright 2020. Grace LaJoy Henderson
Written by Grace LaJoy Henderson
Published by Inspirations by Grace LaJoy
Raymore, MO 64083

ISBN: 978-1-7341868-6-4

All rights reserved. No portion of this book may be reproduced, photocopied, stored or transmitted in any form except by prior written approval of the publisher.

Printed in the United States of America

DIARY OF EMOTIONS: THOUGHTS AND FEELINGS
Grace LaJoy Henderson

DEDICATION

To everyone who has read this book before it was published, when it was only a draft. Your feedback was priceless. Thank you for expressing the value you felt this book might have on the lives of others who may be experiencing similar situations and emotions.

ACKNOWLEDGEMENT

The *Finding Mother Series* is my own recollection of my siblings' and my reunion with our mother after forty-nine years. When referring to my father, mother and siblings, I use fictitious names, as this is *my* story to tell. Their accounts may be different, as they may have perceived things from a different angle.

ABOUT THE SERIES

The *Finding Mother Series* is a complex, touching opportunity for readers to see into the author's journey to find her mother after decades. This series would be ideal for students at a secondary level who are searching for insight about the emotional conflicts and battles one must face when someone they care about has a mental illness. The four books in the series are segmented to provide specific lenses to the overall process, with a number of opportunities available for opening discussions about mental illness from both the author's point of view and her mother's.
~Leslie Arambula, MA Creative Writing, English Teacher

DIARY OF EMOTIONS: THOUGHTS AND FEELINGS
Grace LaJoy Henderson

A WORD FROM THE AUTHOR
ABOUT THE FINDING MOTHER SERIES

Stories like mine are common and there is a sincere need to establish dialogue concerning this issue.

When I asked my mother how she felt about me publishing our reunion story, she laughed and said, "I guess it will be alright." Then she laughed again. She seemed flattered. Therefore, I really want her to feel proud about the way I present my recollection of the story. I told her I would not be revealing her real name or location.

To protect my mother's privacy, I have not revealed the full name under which she was found. I would never have found her under the name listed in my original foster care storybook. I believe that my personal recollection of our reunion details will inspire you. I hope it will decrease the stigma of mental illness in order to promote helpful discussion about this subject.

Due to my own personal struggle with the stigma surrounding mental illness, initially, I was only going to share the positive details of finding and reuniting with my mother. I did not intend to share any of the parts that were embarrassing for me. However, when others heard my story of how I found my mother after five decades, they told me they felt inspired. Many had similar stories. Realizing my personal story was intriguing, and could be helpful to so many people, I am sharing it…all of it.

DIARY OF EMOTIONS: THOUGHTS AND FEELINGS
Grace LaJoy Henderson

TABLE OF CONTENTS

FOREWORD – PHYLLIS HARRIS, FORMER MISSOURI STATE DIRECTOR **9**

FOREWORD – JACOB KELOW, SECONDARY SCHOOL COUNSELOR **10**

PREFACE   **11**

INTRODUCTION   **13**

AFTER MY SECOND TRIP   15

July 20, 2018

August 11, 2018

August 11, 2018 – Addendum

August 12, 2018

August 22, 2018

August 22, 2018

September 9, 2018

September 12, 2018

September 15, 2018

September 16, 2018

September 17, 2018

September 30, 2018

October 5, 2018

October 6, 2018

October 8, 2018

October 26, 2018

Table of Contents Continued →

DIARY OF EMOTIONS: THOUGHTS AND FEELINGS
Grace LaJoy Henderson

TABLE OF CONTENTS (CONTINUED)

November 1, 2018
November 20, 2018
November 22, 2018
December 1, 2018
January 23, 2019
January 23, 2019
April 20, 2019
April 28, 2019
May 12, 2019
May 13, 2019
June 16, 2019
August 6, 2019
September 15, 2019
September 22, 2019
September 24, 2019

IN CLOSING	**101**
DISCUSSION QUESTIONS	**102**
QUESTIONS TEACHERS CAN ASK	**104**
FURTHER DISCUSSION POINTS	**105**
FINDING MOTHER SERIES	**107**
ABOUT THE AUTHOR	**111**

DIARY OF EMOTIONS: THOUGHTS AND FEELINGS
Grace LaJoy Henderson

FOREWORD

Nobody likes to "hurry up and wait." However, life events can keep us stagnant. This is the current quandary of the author. This book is appropriately entitled *Diary of Emotions: Thoughts and Feelings*. In this book, the author goes through an up and down, back and forth, tug of war between her heart and her head. She is in a perpetual "She loves me, she loves me not" emotional pattern as she strives to discern her mother's true feelings.

She found her mentally ill mother after 49 years and desires to take care of her. However, she cannot get her mother to move to Kansas City, so that she and her siblings can tend to her needs and improve the quality of her life. It seems her mother is so used to living in a state of poverty, that living in abundance scares her. The author is struggling with the challenges of maintaining this type of long-distance connection.

The entries in this diary reveal that the author is experiencing a very natural stage of the new relationship with her mother. Enough time has not passed for her to be able to accept the reality of who her mother really is. It seems she desires a "typical" mother-daughter relationship, but may never have it due to her mother's condition. This leaves the author feeling impatient and, at times, overwhelmed.

It seems closure is nowhere in sight for the author at this time. Therefore, she continues to go through a very common thought process that many of us go through when a life circumstance disappoints us.

This diary is a very interesting and enjoyable read. It is an excellent window for people to look into the author's heart. It can help readers learn to open windows of their own souls in the midst of challenging life experiences. The book is full of anticipation for the author and her mother to permanently connect in a way that ensures positive outcomes!

~**Phyllis Harris, Former Missouri State Director**
Parent Information Resource Center

DIARY OF EMOTIONS: THOUGHTS AND FEELINGS
Grace LaJoy Henderson

FOREWORD

As a school counselor, students come into my office everyday who struggle with emotion management. A significant part of their struggle is that they feel alone as they maneuver through tough times. They think they are the only ones who are confused about how they should feel.

Diary of Emotions: Thoughts and Feelings demonstrates that we all are subject to endure emotional turmoil at some point in our lives. It illustrates that it is okay to be confused or unsure.

Although we believe things will work out in the end, it is necessary that we give ourselves the time and space to feel these emotions no matter how conflicting or difficult they may be.

I definitely believe that this book could benefit secondary school students.

~**Jacob Kelow, M.S.Ed.**
Secondary School Counselor
Kansas City Public Schools

DIARY OF EMOTIONS: THOUGHTS AND FEELINGS
Grace LaJoy Henderson

PREFACE

In *Diary of Emotions,* I delve into the depths of my heart to give you a detailed account about my inner turmoil as well as my mixed feelings about my mother. Having forgiven my mother a long time ago, I strive to make her happy while trying to protect my own heart and soul against the challenge that is a mother suffering from mental illness.

DIARY OF EMOTIONS: THOUGHTS AND FEELINGS
Grace LaJoy Henderson

DIARY OF EMOTIONS: THOUGHTS AND FEELINGS
Grace LaJoy Henderson

INTRODUCTION

Hopefully by now, you have read my foster care story and the other three books in the *Finding Mother Series*, all of which have led up to the thoughts and feelings I share in this one.

The thread throughout this book seems to be me toiling with: Should I stop calling my mother? Should I continue sending packages to her? There are sensible reasons to justify stopping both the calls and the packages. However, there are also justifications to continue. So far, I have kept on because a part of me feels like it would be wrong to stop, knowing that she has a mental illness and she may actually need my consistency regardless of how I feel about it.

It is hard to imagine stopping entirely, but I am strongly considering it. The things I have sent lately have either been lost in the mail or stolen by my mother's housemates. That has discouraged me from wanting to send things. Then, couple that with the fact she may not come to the phone, or call me, to confirm whether she received what I have sent. Overall, regardless of what I decide, I will be forever grateful that I found her and that I know where she is.

When I first began journaling, I expressed myself in my audio recorder. Later, I transcribed the audio recordings onto paper. Then, I carefully edited each one. The entries will reveal the way I went back and forth in my thoughts and feelings, as I pondered everything I had learned since finding my mother. In order to keep my true intended tone of voice, this book may feature some improper grammar and sentence structure. Since this is a "diary," I wanted to preserve the way I actually spoke, and not remove it during the editing process.

I believe readers will be interested in my thoughts and feelings because they will be able to understand, relate to, and analyze them. So, travel with me into an array of thoughts and feelings as you read my *Diary of Emotions.*

DIARY OF EMOTIONS: THOUGHTS AND FEELINGS
Grace LaJoy Henderson

AFTER MY SECOND TRIP

When I returned home from the second trip to visit my mother, I kept in close contact with her counselor, Rashad. He and I talked about the release of information form that he had asked me to sign so that he would be able to talk openly with me about my mother. He calmed my concerns by explaining that he did not expect me to take any major responsibility for her.

The form would just allow me to be able to call and learn how she is doing or if she needs anything. I finally decided to sign the paper. However, when I picked up the form to sign it, I realized it was not my signature he needed, but hers. She was the one who needed to grant permission for him to talk to me. I went ahead and signed it per his request, then he also obtained her signature.

Rashad answered his phone whenever I called and he was always available. He listened attentively whenever I spoke. He provided me with great insight about my mother's mental condition.

I appreciated him so much, until finally one day I called him on his cell phone and he informed me he was no longer working for the center. He had been fired because, while he was great when it came to communicating with families, he struggled with some of the other aspects of social work, like documentation of the patient files. I told him how great I thought he was and that

DIARY OF EMOTIONS: THOUGHTS AND FEELINGS
Grace LaJoy Henderson

I would miss him. He was very knowledgeable about how to interact with families who are going through a crisis. Needless to say, I was saddened to learn of his departure. He was the only one who had actually answered his phone.

Before I met the center staff, I used to call the office numbers, but the phones constantly went unanswered. When I met the center manager, Donna, she told me no one ever answers the office phone and gave me her cell phone number. I felt like I would finally be able to call and actually talk to someone. After going back home to Kansas City, she answered my call twice and then she stopped altogether. Therefore, at this time, I have no one at the mental health treatment center to talk to about my mother's status. The boarding home staff are still available, however.

When I returned home from the second trip, Elsie had not yet given me the results from searching my siblings' names and dates of birth. Therefore, I sent a revised email to her including the new hospital information. With this additional information, I was feeling more and more encouraged that she would be able to locate my siblings in her database.

However, one week later, Elsie finally sent me a response letting me know that her agency did not handle any adoptions for my siblings. She told me that another agency might have handled their adoptions. I felt surprised, yet disappointed, that even with all of the information I had, she was still unable to locate them in her database. However, as she said, another agency may have handled their adoption. For now, I have given up on searching for the four children my mother had after she left.

DIARY OF EMOTIONS: THOUGHTS AND FEELINGS
Grace LaJoy Henderson

DIARY OF EMOTIONS: THOUGHTS AND FEELINGS
Grace LaJoy Henderson

July 20, 2018

It is weird that my mother can leave me and I can still forgive her. Or have I really forgiven her? That is another issue, I guess. I feel like maybe I have forgiven her. Pretty much for years, I had *totally* forgiven her. I did not blame her for anything. However, now I have met her and it appears she actually did not want us.

Seeing that she does not want to be with us, I feel like I should place some of the blame on her. I know she was not capable of raising us, but even knowing that, it still makes me want to accuse her of something. I feel like, "How does a mother just abandon her children and not want come be with them when they find her?" Well, she has a mental illness and that is how she can do that.

Still it hurts that my mother has mental problems to the point where she does not want her children. Yet she seems so alert, like she understands life.

Her mental illness has been diagnosed so obviously it is real.

Still, I do not know how to feel about her. I sent her some things, and I guess that is all I really want, is just to be able to send her some things when I feel like it. A part of me wants to do things for her all the time, to take care her. It seems she sees me as like a friend I guess; or maybe she sees me as more than a friend. I do not know. It is hard to fathom how a mother could not want to be close to her children. Like if I do not call her, we do not talk. If I stopped calling her, I would never hear from her again, even though she has my phone number. Then again, it may be for the best.

DIARY OF EMOTIONS: THOUGHTS AND FEELINGS
Grace LaJoy Henderson

August 11, 2018

I called my mother today and she did not come to the phone. It has been a few weeks since the last time we talked because I had been feeling like she would rather be to herself. In the past, it seemed like she wanted to say she did not feel like talking, but she never said it. She always came to the phone.

This is the time when I least expected it and this is when it finally happened. I just hope she is ok. Perhaps she has not been taking her medication, and that could be why she did not want to converse with anybody. That would be my only concern, because she always acts like she wants to talk when I call her.

She may just be more comfortable not communicating with anybody since she has been on her own for so long. I have always suspected that, but every time I called, it seemed like she was happy to speak with me, happy that I called, so I did not want to *not* call her and leave her wondering, "Why isn't anybody calling me?" However, if she does not really care to hear from anybody then, I am okay with not calling her.

The last time I called, she came to the phone. She was saying she had to get off the phone for some reason, which was unclear. However, a couple of moments later she said, "I enjoy it when you call." I felt like maybe that might have been her way of saying, "Even though I enjoy these phone calls, I just do not care much for being on the phone." Furthermore, whenever we are on the phone, she says, "Well, yeah, I was sleeping," or "I was in my room getting my clothes ready for the week."

I'll say, "Okay then, I will not keep you."

But, then she'll say, "So, how have you been doing?" kind of like she does not really care to talk but she does not want to hurt my feelings.

I have always sort of felt like maybe she preferred not to be on the phone. I guess she is not going to say how she really feels. She is not going to tell me she does not want to talk to me because we found after almost fifty years.

Like, how do you tell your daughter, "I really do not need to talk to you?"

It would be okay if she said that to me because it would help me; and that way I would not call because I would understand where she is coming from and how she feels. That way we would have an understanding, as opposed to just acting it out.

I just did not want her to feel like nobody was calling her. I am okay with not calling her considering I do not know her that well and there is not really anything I need from a mother. The only thing I really needed was to hear her tell me why she left in her own words. I needed to know if she wanted to move to Kansas City. I got the answers I desired, so technically there is nothing else I need.

DIARY OF EMOTIONS: THOUGHTS AND FEELINGS
Grace LaJoy Henderson

It would be nice if she were a mother who I could talk to about things; if I could tell her what I am going through with my sister, who also has a mental illness, and she could say, "Yeah well this is what worked for me and this is what you could do for her."

I just wish I could talk to her about some things but I know that she is on medication and trying to deal with her own inner emotions, thoughts, and feelings; and trying to keep from cussing people out when they do stuff to her. She is just not capable of doing anything for anyone.

For instance, when Arica and I were visiting with her she said, "That is just somebody else wanting something from me." I do not remember why she made that statement. But, it made me feel like she feels people just want things from her, and I think the bottom line is she is just not able to give anything.

It does feel nice to talk with her when she shares what is on her mind. I do not necessarily need that because I have been without her for so long. Even though I know where she is, I also know she is not able to have the kind of relationship with me that I would want from a mother. I guess a part of me wants to support her in a bigger way, but when I call her and she says she does not feel like talking to anyone, well then, I feel like I should just let her have her life, you know?

Why should I force anything if she is happy with her life?

DIARY OF EMOTIONS: THOUGHTS AND FEELINGS
Grace LaJoy Henderson

I would like to send her *something*, but only on special occasions. Not like a long-standing relationship. Maybe not talk to her every other week or so but, only if it is like Christmas, Mother's Day or her birthday, just to acknowledge her.

It is kind of a cool knowing where she is and knowing that she is okay, finally, after all these years, and having a sincere understanding that she is just not able to be a mother.

I realize there is a lot I still do not know about her. Yet, I feel a sense of responsibility for her just because she gave birth to me. However, she left me in the hospital and my dad had to take me home. That makes me question my sense of responsibility.

However, I do not foresee it vanishing, because I intend to send her some things soon. Maybe some pants, maybe a winter coat. She could probably use some long socks, especially with the winter months coming up; maybe a sweater or two. Maybe a turban to wear on her head. I think she would appreciate it, but I also think she is content, even if I do not send her things.

I do not know whether I should send her a coat. She mentioned wanting to have a coat with some pockets on the inside. However, I know that she has the means to keep warm because it was cold outside when we were there, and she was wearing that leather coat and black hat, and she had on her little tennis shoes. She was warm and her needs were met.

DIARY OF EMOTIONS: THOUGHTS AND FEELINGS
Grace LaJoy Henderson

I do not know if she would wear the turban, but you never know. The turban might be too much for her. She might think, "this is too flashy." However, I think she would be okay with some socks. I will probably send her some socks. Maybe some under shirts and maybe a few dollars.

She might like a new hat, since she always wears that black one. I may get her some boots for her birthday or Christmas. That would be nice. I think she would like them. They would be comfortable and I think she would enjoy them for the winter.

Well, that is all. I just wanted to talk about my mother for a few minutes, because I just called her and finally, she said she does not feel like talking to anybody. I have always expected that, but when it finally happened, it made me feel sad. I just needed to vent about it.

August 11, 2018 – *Addendum added on May 16, 2019*

I *did* feel hurt when she did not come to the phone. It was like she did not want us then and she does not want us now. I even processed how I was feeling at that time with my brother, Jerome. He encouraged me to just take her word and believe that she just was not feeling up to coming to the phone.

After all, the worker there told me she was okay, but her hip was hurting. Although that made good sense, all the rejection

DIARY OF EMOTIONS: THOUGHTS AND FEELINGS
Grace LaJoy Henderson

that I felt over the years came rushing back and overruled the part that made sense.

That was one of the days when I was convinced, telling myself that, "I guess she *really* did not want us."

August 12, 2018

Just thinking about my mother and a part of me says that is cool if she does not to be with us, I haven't been with her all my life anyway. I know she has a mental illness, and that she is happy where she is. I feel like the biggest part of me does not really care. Then, there is that part of me that does care and that is the part of me that is talking right now.

She is in another state and I would love to be able to take care of her by making sure she gets treatment for her hip because she is always in pain. She said she had an x-ray, but never got the results and I believe she cares about herself. She has mentioned wanting to get the care she needs for her hip. It is just that there is nobody taking care of her so she is just walking around with the pain, not really knowing or understanding what is really going on inside of her body.

I wish I could do something about it. For example, I was looking online and saw a hip brace that she can wear around her hip and her leg for support. Then again, what good will a brace do if we are not aware of what is really going on, we do not have a diagnosis.

I am sure it would give her some support and help her to feel better when she walks. I could send her one of those and let her get used to wearing it for a while. Then maybe send another one later when that one wears out. However, it would be nice if I could actually facilitate getting her the medical care she needs.

I do not know if the boarding home takes care of the residents in that way there. I guess I could call and ask, but I do not think that would be a good idea. My mother knows how to express her own wants and needs. If she wants medical care, I am sure she will ask for it.

One might think it would be easy for me to simply say, "I don't care," since she has been gone for so many years. However, that is not the case. I understand that her mental illness caused her to be away, and that it prevents her from fully showing that she cares.

I believe she cares about family, but not enough to want to live close to us. She loved it when we went to visit her, she could not wait until we got there and she was happy the entire time that we were there. She spent a lot of time with us and was very elated to have us there.

It is just hard to really look after her when she is living there. She is so used to taking care of herself, that I have wondered if she could be afraid to be with us. Because when I mentioned that the place I had in mind for her here would make sure she takes her medication, I noticed she seemed a bit fearful, as if she does not want anyone making sure she takes it.

DIARY OF EMOTIONS: THOUGHTS AND FEELINGS
Grace LaJoy Henderson

If I was retired and home all day, I probably would want to take care of her. I could spend time with her. I could take her to the park. I could take her out walking. I could oversee her healthcare. I could just take care of her.

I do not know if they have any mental health treatment centers here like the one she attends.

If she lived with me, I would make sure she has healthy meals, but then she would need to go to some type mental health treatment center all day long when I go to work. Even when I do not go to work, she could go there and get her mental health needs taken care of.

That looks like a good place where she is currently at, offering her the behavioral health care that she needs every single day like that. I do not know of any places like that here where she could actually have that. The boarding home where she is living is not so cool. However, she goes to the center, which seems like a nice place for her to go.

Nevertheless, there is still that feeling of sadness that comes with having met her and she does not want to be with us. She did not even come to the phone yesterday.

I feel like I am not supposed to care.

I feel like I should not care.

A part of me does not.

Then again, I do.

DIARY OF EMOTIONS: THOUGHTS AND FEELINGS
Grace LaJoy Henderson

It is like, I cannot even really have a mother to talk to on the phone. I know she has a mental illness. However, that does not change the disappointment that comes from not being able to have the type of relationship that I would expect I should have with someone who is my mother.

She is so little and such a nice person. I feel badly because she has had to deal with a mental illness for most of her life. I feel badly that she did not have her children in her life.

She did not have her husband, my father, whom she seemed to really look up to and admire.

She said, "He never came" to visit her in the mental hospital, where she stayed for two years. The thought of him never coming makes me feel sad. Her mental illness caused her not to have her family.

It is kind of like she probably would have wanted a family if somebody was taking care of her. My father was not really equipped to take care of mental issues. He needed her to take care of him, the house, and the children. They needed each other, but neither was able to fulfill the needs of the other.

In a way, she may not have allowed him to be able to care for her because she might have been in denial about taking her medication. If he could not get her to take it, then how could he help her to manage her mental illness? I have seen how my sister is, and sometimes you cannot really control a person who has a mental illness.

While a part of me feels like my father should have taken care of her and given her the medication. Another part of me knows my father may not have had that kind of control over my mother.

After she went off to the mental hospital, my father was trying to work and take care of us and I guess he couldn't have the time off to go and visit my mother, especially if he was feeling unwanted. He may have thought, "Why should I push myself upon her?"

Even now, she is in a good place, but I feel like I have to "pursue" her just to be able to talk to her and do things for her. My father would probably have had to push himself upon her even more so back then. According to my brother, she was in a much worse place back then. I would imagine if she is reluctant to take medication now, she was probably even more reluctant back then.

My father had to call the police to have her committed to a mental hospital. So, I guess that would indicate that she may not have been taking her medication like she should and he could not get her to cooperate so that she could be okay. So, once he got her placed in the mental hospital, he may have just proceeded with his life of raising six children. Keeping track of her progress may have been too much for him.

DIARY OF EMOTIONS: THOUGHTS AND FEELINGS
Grace LaJoy Henderson

My father said she could be the sweetest person, but then she could be the total opposite. When this happened, there was really no getting through to her. I guess I can imagine why my father "never came." It is sad and it seems like, "Oh that is too bad. Nobody ever came," you know?

If she were in a mental hospital here, I think I would go visit her because they would be keeping her on her medication. My father was probably not up to taking care of her when he needed so much help himself, that is just my guess.

Anyway, I thank God for my Grandmother. She was there for us, and during my time with her, I saw what it looked like to have a good, decent, normal life. The places where I lived with my father were not so nice. Many times, we did not have food and almost never had a phone. We would have a phone for a short period, then it would get disconnected since no one paid the bill.

I do not remember our utilities being turned off while my father was around. But, after he left us in the house alone, the utilities were disconnected due to nonpayment. I remember not having a phone even with my father around. I remember thinking, "When I grow up and get my own place, I am going to *always* have a phone, and my bills will *always* be paid."

After my mother left, my grandmother came to see about us a lot. Whenever I was over at my grandmother's house, I had a decent life. I appreciate my grandmother. I have always had nothing but love for her.

Whenever I went to my grandmother's house, there was always food. She brought homemade milkshakes, which she made in the blender, to my bedside before I would go to sleep at night. I guess milk does help people to fall asleep. Sometimes the milkshake would be strawberry, sometimes it would be chocolate, and sometimes it would be vanilla. Strawberry was my favorite!

She showed me what it was like to have all the necessities and a fulfilled life; and what it was like to have someone to really, really look out for me. She completely looked out for me, she took care of me, and all of my needs: physical and social.

She took me places, like out of town with her. She enrolled me in school and drove me to kindergarten when I was only four years old. My grandmother had taught me my ABCs, numbers, and shapes. Therefore, the school let me enroll early because I had taken the early entrance test.

Grandmother would never allow me to eat at fast food restaurants. It was she who showed me what it was really like for someone to be nice to you, to have everything you want and need, to have somebody teach you the things that you need, to buy you toys that are fun and educational. She was the only one who taught me what it felt like to be a well-rounded person. I credit her for that. I would not have even known what all of that looked like had it not been for her.

I want to say, I was not with her long enough to reap the full benefits; but then again, my mother was with her all of her life, and my mother still ended up dealing with mental illness, and becoming opposite of what my grandmother taught her. Therefore, I am not sure if the amount of time I was with her is relevant.

Yeah, it would be nice to have my mother here, so that I could serve her some heathy meals and oversee her medication. I could get her the care she needs for her hip. I could take her to her medical appointments. Maybe in addition to taking her out for walks, I could take her to the park. I could take her to get her hair done, to get manicures and pedicures, take her to church. It is nice to think about all the ways I could take care of her, but it seems she is doing fine right where she is.

It sounds like she could possibly have her own room at the place where she is right now if she could live on the second floor. But, she needs to be on the first-floor due to her hip pain.

I guess she does not necessarily have to be here in Kansas City with us. If she just had her own room then maybe she would not have to carry her stuff around. What are the chances of her getting her own room though? I wish there was a way that I could make things better for her while she is there, but that would just be a lot for me to take on.

DIARY OF EMOTIONS: THOUGHTS AND FEELINGS
Grace LaJoy Henderson

Maybe I will just go ahead and send her the hip brace. I do not know if that will work for her or not. I wish she knew what was going on in her hip area. It could be arthritis and she could possibly need surgery. It could be just a matter of physical therapy and she could be all better. I guess she needs to find out the results of the x-ray that she had. If she only needs physical therapy then the brace may actually be helpful.

Anyway, enough of that. I do not know if I want to initiate taking on responsibility for her. Especially since she has not requested it…also, since she does not want to be with us, *and* since she does not really care to come to the phone when I call. Anyway, that is all I need to say for now.

DIARY OF EMOTIONS: THOUGHTS AND FEELINGS
Grace LaJoy Henderson

August 22, 2018

I would really be happy to learn more about my mother's life story. I was reading my foster care story, *A Gifted Child in Foster Care*, for the first time since finding my mother. As I read the book, I was just kind of reminiscing on how I felt as I wrote that story, compared to how I feel now after meeting my mother. I was reading some of the things I wrote about her, the things I remember when I was only two, and then thinking about her now and trying to imagine her actually doing those things that I remember.

I even wrote a part in the book about never being able to find her and finally giving up, because I really had given up. I truly did not think I would be able to find her at the time that I wrote my foster care story.

Finding her has just put a completely different view on the situation. I have peace, contentment, and comfort; and I feel empowered. All of those things just for finding her and seeing who she really is, and getting a good look for myself at her mental illness that she had before she left, that I did not even recognize back then.

For example, in my foster care story, I did not know why she seemed so "slow" and told me that I had to take a bath before I could have those cookies that she made, but then it seemed like she did not even care, or have any motivation, to make sure I got any of the cookies. I mean, she did not put any aside for me, and she gave me my bath so slow and she left all the cookies with all of the other children. She did not seem to have any understanding that I probably was not going to get any of those cookies even though she told me I could have some after I took my bath.

Seeing her now helps me to understand that. It is like "Okay, now I see," but at the time it just did not make sense to me why I missed out on those cookies.

I still cannot believe that woman is my mother. However, like I said, I want to learn more about her life story. I would like to put the pieces together and learn about her life as a little girl. Like, when did she realize she had mental illness? I would really like to know her story.

The question is, will I be able to get the pieces that I need in order to know her story?

Will she talk to me?

Is she able open up to me?

Because when it comes to things that are stressful, and things about her life, she closes up and she does not like to talk about it. Then again, maybe her life has not been as stressful as I may think.

She said she was married for two years after she left us and I am wondering what happened after that. She still has that man's last name.

Did they just leave each other but stayed married?

Did she get a divorce and keep his name?

Did he remarry?

Did he have more kids?

I would really like to know more.

I mean she just might open up. It may be therapeutic for her to talk more about her life. She may get a sense of peace from talking about it.

I would like to learn more about her story from a little girl until adulthood, including from the time she left us until where she is today.

I know some things, but there is so much that is still missing.

DIARY OF EMOTIONS: THOUGHTS AND FEELINGS
Grace LaJoy Henderson

August 22, 2018

What do I actually know about my mother's story? From what I gather, my mother was adopted when she was two years old. Her birth mother had about seven children and she was not taking care of any of them because she had a mental illness. The state had taken them all way. My mother was the only one still living with her.

My grandmother told me that my mother's mother did not want her, and she told my grandmother to "take her." So, my grandmother took her. Knowing her mother had the same illness as her, I understand why Grandmother would just take her like that. My mother probably would have ended up in foster care or adopted by somebody anyway.

Now it all makes sense. I believe my grandmother did what she had to do in the situation. She could not have children of her own. She saw this cute little neglected girl, and took the steps necessary to have this little girl so she could take care of her.

My grandmother took care of my mother and it sounds like she treated my mother similar to how she treated me. She taught her things, like how to play the piano. Grandmother always bragged that my mother was a great piano player and that she was smart. Grandmother dressed her up and took all kind of pictures of her.

DIARY OF EMOTIONS: THOUGHTS AND FEELINGS
Grace LaJoy Henderson

I know the city and state where my mother was born and where she grew up. She even remembers the address of where they lived. She grew up with her blood uncle and his wife, which is the woman whom I called Grandmother. She called her uncle Father and she called my grandmother Mother.

My grandmother raised my mother properly. She taught her proper etiquette for all occasions. My grandmother wanted her to be "just as good as anyone else." She had to dress nice, look nice, and talk using correct grammar. That is how my grandmother taught me, too. My Grandmother raised my mother similar to how she raised me during the times I spent with her.

My mother grew up with my grandmother. I did not know any other details about how she grew up except she was wonderful at playing the piano, and my grandmother raised her to be very prim and proper.

After I found my mother, she told me some additional stories about her life. She told me the story of how she met my father, among other stories (which I have shared in the *Finding Mother Series* of books).

I do not know at what point she began to display her mental illness, or when my father learned about it. Did he notice it? Had it begun to show itself around the time they first met? I know she was a pretty woman though, so maybe he could not tell. Maybe it had not manifested during that time. She may have looked so

DIARY OF EMOTIONS: THOUGHTS AND FEELINGS
Grace LaJoy Henderson

"normal" back then that he just could not imagine she would have a mental illness and that it could be so serious. That could be the case.

I would like to know about her life from the time she lived with my grandmother until the time she married my father. When did it become obvious that she had a mental illness to the point that it was affecting her life in such a major way? I would really like to know that.

So anyway, she met my dad and, at some point, they got married. I do not know the details of their dating process, from after their meeting up until their marriage. The next thing I know about my mother is that she married my father and they moved around a lot. As they moved from place to place, they had Jerome, then Grayson, Carla, Terrance, and Danisha. Then I was born.

They ended up in Kansas City, to be close to my grandmother. They needed her help because, by that time, my mother's mental illness was adversely affecting the family. Kansas City is where my mother ultimately ran away from, leaving my father to raise six children alone.

According to my father, she never took her birth control pills the way she should have. He was upset about that. He often complained after she left that she did not believe in birth control and she did not believe in abortion, yet she never wanted that many children.

DIARY OF EMOTIONS: THOUGHTS AND FEELINGS
Grace LaJoy Henderson

During my second visit with my mother, she told me she was on birth control pills but she still ended up pregnant time after time. She ultimately gave birth to ten children. Six with my father and four with Calvin, the man she ran away with.

On another note, she told me a story of something that had happened before she left us. One day when she came home on a furlough from the mental hospital, her children were all telling her that my father had brought a girlfriend over. She said she never said anything to him about it. Her story made me feel like she suspected my father of cheating but she never asked him about it.

She said she never questioned him about what he did when he was away from home either. She said she just loved him and that she taught her children to love him too, no matter what. She told me she learned a long time ago that if you looked for trouble you would find it. Therefore, she never looked for anything bad because he was good to her so she just appreciated that. I was surprised to hear her say that. I felt like that was her way of using wisdom.

My mom seems like she was nonchalant and did not worry about her relationship with my father. It seems she just enjoyed her marriage. It seems she relished the good part and ignored the bad part. I do not know if that is good or bad but that is how she dealt with it. Sadly, she ended up losing my father anyway because

DIARY OF EMOTIONS: THOUGHTS AND FEELINGS
Grace LaJoy Henderson

he put her in a mental hospital and never came back to visit her. I feel disappointed in my father for doing that.

On a side note, during my second visit with my mother, she mentioned she had some good children; she mentioned how Carla was "as cute as a button" when she was born; she mentioned how I was a "real fat baby" and how I was "the cutest thing you ever want to see" when I was born. However, she did not mention any specific details about the births of the rest of my siblings.

I am curious about the details, including her thoughts and feelings, surrounding their births. It is my understanding that Danisha and I would have ended up in foster care or adopted if my father had not been there to take us home from the hospital.

Perhaps I could learn more about my sibling's births, as well of other aspects of my mother's life, if she and I could have more conversations.

DIARY OF EMOTIONS: THOUGHTS AND FEELINGS
Grace LaJoy Henderson

September 9, 2018

So, I am in my feelings about the last time I called my mother and she said she did not feel like talking to anybody. This brings back memories of how my father would tell us that my mother probably would not receive us if we ever found her.

It pains me to admit that he was right. She did not receive us when we first got there. She receives us now, but it is weird because she still seems satisfied without us. She has done a pretty good job trying to make me feel comfortable and trying to make me feel like she actually wants me.

I think she is okay either way. What I mean is, if I want to be in her life, she is okay with it. If I do not, she would be okay with that, too, because she is content the way she is. She left for a reason. She never wanted all of those children. Therefore, she is cool without us at this stage of her life.

In all actuality, I pretty much feel the same way. Even though I am feeling emotional about this, there is still that part of me that feels like she has not been in my life for all of these years, so I am perfectly okay with her not being in my life now.

DIARY OF EMOTIONS: THOUGHTS AND FEELINGS
Grace LaJoy Henderson

September 12, 2018

I am remembering how my mother told me that she volunteered in the children's nursery at the church we used to go to before she abandoned us. For years, I had been sharing a story of how she would come to pick me up from the nursery, and brag to the people there about how smart I was. After I reunited with her, I told her I remembered that story and she confirmed that she actually *volunteered* in the children' nursery. So, she was not merely picking me up.

All of those years when I thought she was picking me up from the nursery, she was actually in there with me because she was volunteering. Even though I vividly remember things about my mother when I was only two years old, there are still parts I do not know. I never would have imagined that she actually volunteered in the nursery.

She does not remember some of the stories that I shared with her. She actually did not even remember the story of bragging about me to the nursery workers. She just remembered that she volunteered in the nursery.

When I asked her if she remembered walking me around to the convenience store and buying me malt balls candy, she did not remember that. She did not remember walking me to the store at all.

DIARY OF EMOTIONS: THOUGHTS AND FEELINGS
Grace LaJoy Henderson

I told her I remembered her laying in the grass in the backyard crying, afraid of being taken away. She did not really respond to that. Probably because it was a hurtful moment, and she preferred to talk about things that felt good to her. She has a way of blocking out negative things and only thinking about good and positive things. That seems to be her way of coping with potentially hurtful things in her life.

It is interesting for me to learn her side of some of the memories I have carried around with me for so many years.

I am also thinking about how my mother mentioned wanting to have a coat with pockets on the inside so that she can hide her stuff. That makes sense since she has been robbed. She also mentioned wanting a cell phone and being able to hide it inside of the coat pockets. She probably would hide it and take good care of it.

However, I am still afraid she might lose it or somebody in the boarding home may steal it while she is asleep, or something, because they would know she has it. I am also concerned about her learning how to use it, because it is not the same as using a regular phone. I do not know if she has ever had one before or if she knows anything about how one works. I know that she would really like to have one. However, I do not know if it is a good idea for me to buy her one.

DIARY OF EMOTIONS: THOUGHTS AND FEELINGS
Grace LaJoy Henderson

She may be better off obtaining a cell phone from one of those places that provide free cell phones for people who are on a fixed income. Sometimes, those places will provide a phone with a certain number of free minutes per month. That could be an option for her to get started with having a phone, since it is free and we could see how she does with it. I am sure she does not need too many minutes per month anyway.

Now I know for sure that the boarding home will let her call her family long distance from there if she wants to. She just chooses not to. I do not know if they would make a big deal out of it if she did it too much. They probably would.

How do you tell a mentally ill resident they cannot call their family? How do you tell an elderly woman who has lived there for over fifteen years she cannot call her family, especially when all of her income goes to that place?

Well anyway, it would be nice if she had her own room in that place. Then I would probably send her a nice mattress. Maybe even a nice comfortable chair. Those are the things I would want to do for her if she were here, but, not really while she is there.

I guess if she did not have to share a room there, it would not hurt. Since she wants to be there, maybe she could have her own space where residents would not be able to steal from her. Then she can have more without having the worry of her things being stolen. Maybe she could even have a television or a refrigerator in her room.

It would be nice if she could have a better room in the place where she actually wants to be. However, then she would no longer fit in with the other residents at the boarding home. She would no longer have the appearance of someone who is homeless. To me, it just does not seem feasible to provide that type of life for her in the place where she is. That is just not the place to have many things. It's really not.

I wonder if there are any nicer assisted-living homes in her city, where she could live. The only thing about that is that she likes the boarding home and she is used to being there. She probably would not want to live in another place. Considering how she has been conditioned, she could potentially carry all of her belongings around in a backpack even if she moves to an environment where no one steals.

This diary entry started with me talking about her working in the church nursery and how she does not remember the stories that I remember. When I told her about when I used to go into her closet and put on her clothes and shoes, I imagined she may have chastised me for it, because she used to take me out of her closet. Then, as soon as she was not looking, I would go right back in there.

DIARY OF EMOTIONS: THOUGHTS AND FEELINGS
Grace LaJoy Henderson

When I mentioned that memory to her during my visit, she had a look on her face that told me that was not a cute memory for her. It was as if she was thinking, "Oh, you remember that?" Her reaction made me wonder if maybe she disciplined me for it and I just do not remember that part.

I am in awe about how I witnessed my mother being beaten by my father, then listened to her as she denied it forty-nine years later. She made excuses for my father, saying he treated her good. She said he never did anything for her to be angry with him about. When in reality he admitted to beating her and it was not right. It was not fair to her.

Then again, if he hit her for harming us, the way Jerome said, then maybe she understands why he did it and therefore, maybe she honestly is not angry with him. I remember my oldest sister, Carla beating up on our sister, Danisha, who has the same mental illness as my mother, for trying to beat up on me.

So maybe that is just what my family did, protected each other. My father protected us from my mother. He did all he could to protect us, and to try to keep us together. For example, bringing me home from the hospital at birth, when my mother was in the mental hospital. That really was honorable of him.

My foster care caseworker used to tell me that my father really cared about us; and that he was doing all he could to keep us together. I did not understand what she meant back then. Now

DIARY OF EMOTIONS: THOUGHTS AND FEELINGS
Grace LaJoy Henderson

I do. He must have told them the story, like the whole story, including how my mother left me in the hospital.

My father never told me that my mother left me in the hospital and that he brought me home. I had never heard that story. I figured it out when I got my birth records. When I looked at my records, I thought, "Wow, it looks like my father took me home from the hospital!" Then my mother confirmed it when I met her. I had heard he brought Danisha home from the hospital, too.

So now, I can see how he tried to keep us together. I used to wonder how he could have possibly been trying to keep us together if he left us in that house alone, and we ended up in foster care. But, now, I am able to look beyond the fact that he put his big old hands on my little bitty mother, and recognize his sincere efforts to do what he thought was best for his children.

DIARY OF EMOTIONS: THOUGHTS AND FEELINGS
Grace LaJoy Henderson

September 15, 2018

I am feeling kind of upset. I feel like I called my mother too soon from the last time. The last time I called was to let her know I had sent her a package and to tell her to expect it last Thursday. She said she was going to call me Thursday to let me know she received it. She did not call me.

I ended up calling her again today just to confirm the package had arrived. I really did not want to speak to her, but the boarding home worker called her to the phone. I did not want to overwhelm her by the frequency of my calls. She did not call me Thursday but I called her today because I really wanted to know if the package got there okay.

To my dismay, the worker went to get her, then came back to the phone and told me she was not coming to the phone. I said okay and we hung up. A couple of minutes later, I decided to call back to find out why she was not coming to the phone, and another worker answered.

It was April, and she exclaimed, "She needs to come to the phone!" After she had confirmed that I was the daughter who was sending her the package, she sounded infuriated. "Most families of the people here don't care anything about them! I am going to go get her because she needs to come to the phone!"

DIARY OF EMOTIONS: THOUGHTS AND FEELINGS
Grace LaJoy Henderson

After a few moments of silence where April went to get Mother, she came back and explained that my mother could not come because her hip was hurting. But, otherwise she was okay.

A part of me wondered if my mother might be using that as an excuse. However, I know that her hip is always hurting. It could be hurting more now than normal. She could not feel like getting up because of it. That could very well be the case, I guess. I remember when we wanted to take her out for dinner and she was concerned about "hopping" into the restaurant. I took that to mean she was concerned because her hip hurts a lot. I guess she does not have to come to the phone if she is in pain. I should not expect it.

Still, I asked myself, "Is her hip really hurting that badly, or is this a sign that she still does not want me after all of these years?"

What if the true reason that she did not come to the phone was because of her hip pain just like she said? What if she truly just did not feel like getting up walking with so much pain? If that is absolutely the reason then I would have to accept that as her reason.

She said she would call me tomorrow. I do not know if I believe that but I just have to take her word. If she does not call me tomorrow then I will know, "Okay, she did not call me."

DIARY OF EMOTIONS: THOUGHTS AND FEELINGS
Grace LaJoy Henderson

April said she would be sure to have her to call me tomorrow. We will see. Otherwise, I am almost tempted to give up trying to have an ongoing relationship with her. I understand that she has a serious mental illness, but understanding that heartbreaking fact does not stop the pain associated with it.

I remember how father and grandmother told me my mother did not want me. Now, I actually see it for myself. They told me the truth but I did not realize it. I felt disappointed with them for telling me that my mother did not want me. I thought, "How can you just tell a child her mother did not want her?" I thought, there's no way my mother did not want me. I thought they were just telling me that.

No, they were serious. They were telling me the truth. My mother did not want me. I can see that now. I mean, I know she enjoys knowing me. She even made a joke about me when we were looking at pictures during my second visit. We were looking at a picture of Arica and I. She said Arica was very pretty in the picture, then she looked at me in the picture and said, "You are *alright*." Then she laughed and we all laughed. I thought it was cute that she knew how to make that kind of joke and that she was comfortable joking with me in that manner.

I know she doesn't dislike me. She just never wanted so many children, and since she has been on her own for so long, she is happier that way.

DIARY OF EMOTIONS: THOUGHTS AND FEELINGS
Grace LaJoy Henderson

September 16, 2018

I am just lying here on my bed before I fall asleep, contemplating how my mother did not come to the phone when I called yesterday. I had talked to her and told her I sent her a package. She told me she was going to call me when it arrived on Thursday and let me know that she got it. She did not do that.

Then I called her to confirm whether or not it was delivered and she did not come to the phone. I do not know if she got the package. I looked up the tracking number and it looked like the center director, Donna, received the delivery.

So, it looked like it was received. I guess I just wanted to know for sure for if the package actually reached my mother's hands. April had said she would make sure Mother called me today, but I did not receive that call. This makes me wonder if it would be easier if I did not know where she was, than to know where she is and feel unwanted by her.

Once, when I sent her something, she told me it was sweet of me to think of her like that. That made me feel like she did not really see me as her daughter who feels obligated to look after her, but like she saw me as a friend who does not owe her anything. I saw her as my mother, someone who I should be taking care of. She just did not seem to feel the same way.

However, one time we were talking on the phone and I told her I was not feeling well. She immediately started giving me

DIARY OF EMOTIONS: THOUGHTS AND FEELINGS
Grace LaJoy Henderson

pointers about how to take care of myself, you know, like a mother would do. I just said, "Yeah," as if to tell her, "I already know how to take care of myself." I felt surprised that her motherly instinct actually stepped up in that moment.

My first instinct was to feel like I did not need a mother. In a way, I felt honored that she showed that she cared. In another way, it felt unusual for her to act "motherly" towards me after being away for my entire life.

So, I am thinking about how she did not come to the phone and did not call me back as she promised. I am seriously considering not ever calling her again because she does not seem interested. Then again, that may be what happened with her and my father. She said he never came.

I am wondering if he could have possibly felt the same way I am feeling right now, and if that could have possibly been the reason why he gave up on her. I would hate for her to experience the same rejection from me that she experienced from my father. However, I am afraid I may approach another point in my life where I will have to say, "Well, if she don't want me, I don't want her *needer*."

That could also be why neither he, nor my grandmother, took us to visit her in the mental hospital leading up to her disappearance. My father seemed to have known she would not receive us, so taking us to see her might have been more harmful for us than helpful. She may not have really cared to have us visit since, according to her, she was in the hospital because she needed a break from all of her children.

Therefore, taking us to visit her may have been counter-productive for her. Besides, I believe that if she really wanted to see us, she would have come for us after she left the hospital, before running off with Calvin. She also knew the city and state where she left us, so she could have always come back to find us if she wanted.

I believe she actually remembers a whole lot more surrounding the time she ran away from Kansas City. I think she may feel ashamed of not wanting us. She admitted wanting a "break" from us, however. So, I can appreciate her being honest with me about that. Back then, we were little children who may have been a burden to her. It may have been hard for her to imagine, at that time, that we would one day be grown-ups who would no longer need her.

Well anyway, I have a decision to make. I have to decide if I am going to continue to try to reach out to her when it seems as if she does not really care about that. I feel torn between continuing to call her and stopping calling her. I guess I could talk to April about it first. April would probably say, "Just keep calling her," because she needs family even if she does not act as if she does.

DIARY OF EMOTIONS: THOUGHTS AND FEELINGS
Grace LaJoy Henderson

It would be nice for me to be able to call her every once in a while, just to talk to her. It would be nice if I could continue to send her things, just because she is my mother, just because she gave birth to me. However, it would also be nice to be able to confirm she received what I sent, and to know whether she liked it.

For example, I wonder if she likes the yarn and knitting needles I sent. I wonder if she is actually knitting. Maybe when I ask April about whether or not I should continue to call my mother, I can also ask her if the knitting supplies were helpful for her. That is, if she even received the package. I was hoping the knitting supplies could be a source of therapy since her counselor told me she shared her desire to knit in a group therapy session. It would mean a lot to me if she were actually knitting.

However, for the most part, my mission is accomplished. I found her, I know where she is and I know what she is like. She does not seem interested in being a mother or a grandmother. I mean, she told my daughter, Arica, to call her Geneva.

I do not know what it would have been like to grow up with her. I have always wondered, "What would be worse? Her staying in Kansas City, but being in a mental hospital? Her being in the home with us, but doing things to harm us? Never finding her and not knowing anything about her condition? Or finding her after all these years, the way we did, but not really being able to have a relationship with her due to her mental illness?'

I guess my choice would be to know her, but I realize I am not going to have a mother in the way that I would like to.

The least I wanted was some occasional conversation. I originally wanted to talk to her a lot and listen to her talk. I wanted to learn a lot about her life; what she likes and what her life has been like for all the years she has been gone. I learned her story of why she left, but I still do not know where she has been all of these years.

After going back to visit her for a second time and seeing how hard it was for her talk about why she left, I resolved to accept the fact that I may never know what she did with her life from the time she left until the time we found her. I mean, I know she married Calvin. I know she had four more children, all of whom she left in a hospital. I know she mentioned living with a family for eight years.

I wanted to ask her for more details about living with that family, but she did not seem like she wanted to expound on it, so I did not ask. I know that she has been living at the boarding home for over fifteen years now. However, I am oblivious to any other details concerning where she has been since she abandoned us forty-nine years ago. I am guessing she spent many of those years committed to a mental hospital, but I do not really know.

DIARY OF EMOTIONS: THOUGHTS AND FEELINGS
Grace LaJoy Henderson

Our situation is somewhat unfortunate, but at least I was fortunate enough to have found her. For years, I prayed to find her. I always felt in my heart that I would find her one day. I had even had a dream once about my siblings and I going to another state together to reunite with her, and that actually ended up happening!

Therefore, I got my wish, which was to find her before she passed away. I feel like I should just simply be happy with that, especially if she is satisfied where she is and she is okay. She complains about the boarding home residents stealing from her. She is content to be there though and she does not want to leave.

I mean, I have a choice. I can leave her alone and say, "Okay, she is happy," or I can continue to acknowledge her for holidays. I sent the last package "just because." There was no holiday or special occasion. Regardless of what I decide to do, it would still be nice to know how she felt about that last package I sent or if she even received it.

Maybe I will call Donna and ask her, since she would have been the one who gave it to her. I mean, my mother knows how to call me and tell me, but it does not seem like she is going to do that.

As Terrance once said, "It would be nice if *she* would give *us* a call." It would let us know that she wants to talk to us.

I feel like giving up.

DIARY OF EMOTIONS: THOUGHTS AND FEELINGS
Grace LaJoy Henderson

Besides, why should I keep sending her things when people who live with her are just going to steal it from her? If she has many things in a place where other residents have nothing, it would make her a very large target. Therefore, it may actually be best for her, too, if I stop sending stuff.

So anyway, I guess I have said enough for now. Basically, I wanted to talk out my feelings about her not coming to the phone yesterday, her not calling me back like she promised, and about not really knowing the status of the package that I sent.

September 17, 2018

I am having thoughts about my father and the way he acted after my mother left the family. My father was very protective over my siblings and me. Now, I understand why. I now understand his struggle.

Over the years, my oldest brother often shared his own anger about how people treated us and how my father stood up for us. The full details of what my brother shared with me are his own story to tell. However, my point is this: I never fully understood his anger and I never fully understood my father's commitment to us until I met and talked to my mother.

As I was growing up, whenever I would speak of my disappointment about my father beating my mother, my brother would say, "Grace, our mother really did have a mental illness and our father didn't cause it." Even though my brother explained that to me on numerous occasions over the years, I continued to believe that my father was the reason my mother left, and that he somehow caused her mental illness to manifest itself more largely that it would have if it were not for the way he treated her.

I do think she may have lived a better life if she had only had the two children that she wanted, and if my father had not expected more from her as a wife than she was capable of giving. Did he have a right to expect those things? I guess so. I believe we all have our expectations of what we want from a mate and so did my father. Unfortunately, my mother was unable to deliver.

I believe that the pressure from my father for her to deliver caused more stress on her mental condition. It seemed my father did not really understand her mental illness and the full effects of it on a large family. It seems I misunderstood my father's challenge of not having my mother as the helpmate that he so desperately longed for and desired.

When I reviewed my birth records a second time, after finding my mother, I realized the hardship my father must have experienced having to take me home and care for me without the help of my mother.

Mother confirmed she was in a mental hospital when I was born, which is why my father took me home from the hospital. This part really makes me realize the investment my father had in me, how much he cared, how much he loved me, the hardships he experienced just to keep us together, and the pain of not having help from our mother to raise us.

He was already struggling to raise five children with a mentally ill wife, when I was born. Yet he was still committed to bringing me home from the hospital to keep his family together.

Meeting my mother and talking to her has helped me to better understand my father's struggles, his justifications, his hurt, his anger, and why he was so very protective of my siblings and I. He even protected us against our mentally ill mother. I realized my father had a lot vested in me and my siblings, and I now believe that is why my father was so protective of me as I was growing up.

He *always* took my side even when I was wrong. If an outsider came knocking on our door to tell him of something I did wrong, he would tell them they needed to be focusing on their own children instead of telling him about his. I would never get in trouble when outsiders would snitch on me.

However, in my heart, I would feel lucky that my father became angry with them instead of punishing me for what they said I had done and I would be sure, within myself, to do better next time.

I am considering what my father must have went through with my mother, while trying to raise six children. Before meeting her and talking with her, I had always blamed him for her leaving. I understand now. I realize what he went through with our mother.

I thought he was just making excuses when he was talking badly about her, saying how she had mental illness, that she never did anything for us, saying she did not want us, and mocking her for saying, "One day, I am going to go far, far away." Furthermore, how he was afraid that she would not receive us if we ever found her. I had always thought he was just angry. Even though he may have actually been angry in part, I now understand his plight.

When he would say he had to knock some sense into her, I did not understand that. Now I do. I am not saying I agree with him hitting her, but I understand his thought process now.

It is weird because he never physically abused my siblings or me. But, somehow, he thought his beatings would cause her to act the way he wanted her to. He thought that she just needed a good whooping. I guess he thought she was kind of like a child, and that if he just gave her a good whooping that she would do better.

Obviously, that did not work. After meeting and talking with her, it appears she may have understood his actions, because she said he treated her nice.

So maybe he talked with her about it before and after. Maybe she understood that he was hitting her because she had harmed one of us. I have reason to believe he may have also beat her when she did not have dinner ready and the house was dirty when he came home from work.

That is just something I was told. I do not specifically remember that, so it is only hearsay. However, I do remember him complaining about her being home all day and not cooking, cleaning or even getting dressed. I just do not remember if he actually beat her for it.

DIARY OF EMOTIONS: THOUGHTS AND FEELINGS
Grace LaJoy Henderson

Nevertheless, I now understand how my father must have felt to have a wife who had a mental illness, who was not able to be a mother, who was unable do anything for the children, and who did not even want that many children. I wonder if my mother ever imagined that the day would arrive that we would come to reunite with her.

Well, that day came and I am thankful because she finally received us after our very long trip. We had sacrificed way too much to go there to reunite with her, for her to proclaim she did not know who we were.

After she finally accepted us, she said she loves family. I guess a part of her wants family, but a part of her has become satisfied with not having us. The fact that she does not want to come live closer, and the fact that she never initiates phone calls to us, reminds me of how she did not want us back then.

It makes me feel like she still does not want us now.

She may or may not feel that way, but that is how I feel.

However, I am still not sure if the words, "your mother does not want you," were the best thing for my father and grandmother to say to me as a two-year-old child, even if it may have been the truth.

Perhaps something like, "your mother has a mental illness, she does not know how to love you, and she is not able to take care of you," would have been a better way to tell me. Either way I would have felt hurt, so I am not sure if a different wording would have decreased the rejection I felt for most of my life.

Now that I truly understand my father did not in any way cause my mother's mental illness, I am guessing it is simply hereditary because her birth mother had a mental illness. One of my sisters has the exact same mental illness, too.

My father never told my sister she had an illness, and he never sought treatment for her. He just always treated her as if she was very special. I believe he thought he could just be nice to her and she would be okay. His plan did not work. The last time I saw my sister, she was in denial about having a diagnosed mental illness. Therefore, she was not taking any medication to relieve her very serious symptoms.

My feelings still remain mixed.

Should I call my mother again?

Should I just leave her be?

Is she pushing me away because she really wants me to go away?

Would she push me away, then be sad that I am gone?

If I go away, would she feel hurt like nobody cares?

Would it be better for her if I were not pursuing a relationship with her?

DIARY OF EMOTIONS: THOUGHTS AND FEELINGS
Grace LaJoy Henderson

I feel she has been very gracious to us. After all, the only things we ever wanted was to be nice to her, to love her, and take care of her if she would allow it.

On another note, I still want to know what her life was like before she ended up living there.

Did she meet other men after her two-year marriage ended with Calvin?

Had she been homeless on the streets?

Had she been locked away in a mental hospital?

What happened after those two years?

I wish I could ask her.

However, things that happened after she left seemed to be the things that she is most uncomfortable talking about. The good thing about her is that she tries to hold on to all the good memories.

Like the way she stared at the picture of herself standing outside of her childhood home. I am guessing that picture reminded her of the good old days when her life was pleasant. She shies away from talking about hurtful memories.

While finding her has helped me to know more about her than I did before, I still wish I could know more. She seemed to avoid talking too much about Calvin, the man who she ran away with. She said he had family out of town. He, too, had a mental illness but it seems she trusted him to provide for her.

DIARY OF EMOTIONS: THOUGHTS AND FEELINGS
Grace LaJoy Henderson

I guess if she had stayed with us, she would have been expected to be a wife and mother and she did not know how. She would have had to be someone who she was not capable of being.

I believe she saw us, her children, as stressors, burdens. We represented something that caused her grief, something from which she needed to get away.

So, I felt a little bit jealous during my second visit with her. I was sitting in the living room, at the boarding home, talking with my mother. One of the boarding home workers walked into the living room with her son. He looked to be around ten or eleven years old. She walked him over to my mother.

She said, "Geneva, do you remember my son, Tommy?

My mother said, "Oh, wow! Is that Tommy? My how he has grown!"

I was surprised to see this.

The worker was able to share *her* son with *my* mother, who left us as little children. My mother had the capacity to appreciate and enjoy the growth of this little boy.

It really made me feel some kind of a way that this worker knew my mother would be happy to see her son.

It showed me that my mother was a real person, who is able to add joy to the life of someone else, even after running away from her own family.

DIARY OF EMOTIONS: THOUGHTS AND FEELINGS
Grace LaJoy Henderson

September 30, 2018

Taking a moment to appreciate some of the things my brother, Jerome, shared with me about our mother. He told me that when we were growing up, she was excellent with sewing, knitting, cooking, and playing the piano. He said whenever she was taking her medication properly, that she was good at all of those things. He believes she is probably still great at those things today. He does not believe she has lost those special talents. I thought that was interesting.

My grandmother had also told me how talented my mother was. She used to tell me about the piano more than anything else. I do not really remember my grandmother telling me about her sewing, knitting, or cooking. Jerome said our mother's cooking was homemade, from scratch, and delicious!

Knowing those things that she is good at makes me want to bring her to Kansas City and get her involved in those things that she loves, maybe buy her a piano and a sewing machine.

DIARY OF EMOTIONS: THOUGHTS AND FEELINGS
Grace LaJoy Henderson

October 5, 2018

When someone in your family has a mental illness, it is easy to say, "I am going to look past their behavior because I understand that they have a mental illness."

Nevertheless, that does not take away the pain that comes with not having the type of relationship that you would like to have with them.

Sometimes, I wonder what is harder: living without a mother and not knowing her, or knowing her and having to live with the reality of her mental illness.

October 6, 2018

Before I found my mother, I used to think about how horrible it was for me that my mother left and I never knew where she was, and that I did not have a mother.

I used to wonder, why do I have to go through this heart-wrenching situation?

Why me?

Why did this happen to me of all people?

It just did not seem real that this happened to me.

I felt like my mother was not supposed to leave to me, that these types of things only happen to other people and not me.

Sometimes I wonder how my life would have been had I grown up knowing her. What if she would have remained in the mental hospital in Kansas City and I would have been able to visit her periodically?

I believe it may have still been hard not having her at home. I would have likely felt responsible for her, starting at a very young age. Therefore, I think it is better for me that she was out of my life completely. It gave me a chance to have a more normal childhood.

Even still to this day, I sometimes find myself wondering why *my* mother left *me,* why I had to grow up not having a mother, why I still do not have a mother even though I have found her.

DIARY OF EMOTIONS: THOUGHTS AND FEELINGS
Grace LaJoy Henderson

On another note, when she was home, my father could no longer leave us alone with her. She told me how, at one time, he would often go out of town for work, leaving her alone with us. That reminded me of the time when he left my siblings and I in that house alone, so that he could go work in Florida, and we ended up being taken into foster care.

I realize now that was not his first time leaving his family in that manner. In reality, he had stopped traveling for five years (when I was ages two through seven) to stay with us and to try to keep us together. However, that was the first time he left us completely alone, without an adult being in the home with us. So, I am guessing he could not contain his "travel bug" any longer.

On yet another note, I feel disappointed and heartbroken that even though I found my mother, I still do not really have a mother. I believe my brothers realized that immediately, but it took me some time to understand it. I always imagined that she wanted us back then, and that maybe she tried to take us with her.

I sometimes envisioned my father telling her, "You are not taking my children anywhere!"

Causing her to leave without us.

Then I would wonder, "Well, if she wanted us, then why hasn't she tried to find us?" I even imagined that if we ever found her, she would tell us her story and it would sound something like this:

DIARY OF EMOTIONS: THOUGHTS AND FEELINGS
Grace LaJoy Henderson

"Yeah, I did want you all. I tried to take you all with me, but your father would not let me."

Her story was nothing like that.

Her intention was to leave all of us with our father and never have to worry about us again. The good thing, the great thing, the wonderful thing, the blessing is that I was able to find her, to see her, and now my longing has been satisfied.

When I first found her, I was ready to bring her to Kansas City and take care of her without thinking twice about it. Later, when it seemed she was not being clear about whether or not she wanted to come, I began to think about it.

I thought about how, if she were to come, I would be taking care of someone who I do not really know. Someone who did not even want me when I was a little girl. I thought that if she does not want to come, then that would free me from a potentially challenging experience.

Had she agreed to come be with us, I would be taking care of a woman who did not raise me and who was not with me all of my life.

Ironically, however, if she were to call today and say, "I want to come," I would surely begin making arrangements because she is still my mother, so if she actually *wants* to be with us, I would be happy to have her. My brothers and I promised her that if she ever decided to come just let us know and we would make it happen. So, we would keep our promise.

In reality, she does not want to come so I often remind myself that she is in a good place. All of her basic needs are being met. If we had never found her, she would have been okay. I wanted her here with us just in case something serious happened to her then she would be close enough for all of us to be able to help her.

If something serious happens to her while she is there, they may just have to take care of it the way they would if we had not found her. I am grateful to have found her, to have met her, to see what she is like, to have pictures with her, to be able to do some things for her, to have a better understanding of her mental illness and why she left. I am happy to know she is in a stable place where she has been long-term, and she is not living on the streets. I can rest in the fact that this situation is the best it can be.

Now, I am thinking about how my mother did not keep her promise to call me after I sent the package to her.

I know she is very aware of dates, days, and times; and she remembers things very well. Like when Arica and I were scheduled to visit her, she kept asking, "Are you and Arica still coming on June 7th?" Then she would say, "You know Mother's Day is coming up on May 13th?" Then if I called her on a holiday, she would ask, "Are you having a good 4th of July? Did you spend time with your daughter?" Like when Arica and I were there and we came to get her for dinner earlier than she expected, she said, "You all came early." In addition, she gets up in the morning, gets ready for the center, and arrives to the bus on time.

She knows times and days very well.

Therefore, she knows that she said she was going to call me when she got the package and she knows that she did not do it.

After I ended up calling her, she said she would call me back the next day. She did not. When she failed to keep her promises to call me back, I was thinking that maybe her mental illness caused her to forget. In reality, I find it hard to believe that she forgets, which causes me to wonder why she did not call.

That is why I am considering if it would be best for me to simply back away. To think, all my life I had imagined finding my mother and taking care of her.

DIARY OF EMOTIONS: THOUGHTS AND FEELINGS
Grace LaJoy Henderson

October 8, 2018

You know, I could actually cry about my mother, however, I probably will not.

It is difficult finding her, but not really having her. Calling her and her not coming to the phone and not ever calling me.

Over the years, I do not think I have ever cried about not having my mother. I handled my perceived rejection in a different way. My feelings often turned in to heartfelt poems and songs.

I was somewhat silent about it, but I never cried.

Even when they told me she left and did not want me, I did not cry. So why would I start crying about her now? I guess I can think about how unfortunate the situation is. I guess I can allow tears to well up in my eyes. I guess if I ever want to cry, I can just go ahead and do it without holding back.

However, for right now, there is nothing for me to cry about.

I mean, she is okay.

She is a strong woman.

She is probably a lot stronger than I'll ever be in this lifetime. She has been out there. She knows the streets. She was robbed on the streets. Now, she is afraid and I feel sad about that.

That is something I could cry about because I had no idea I would find her living like that. I expected she would be safe and secure in a mental hospital, not able to talk. I never imagined her being out there walking the streets.

She does not really walk the streets anymore.

She is actually living a pretty basic life, going outside on the front step; smoking her cigarettes; eating breakfast, lunch, and dinner; going to bed; getting up; going to the center; talking to people. I mean, she has a real life. She is strong enough to take care of herself.

She looked to my dad to take care of her back then. Then, she looked to Calvin to take care of her when she left. Now, she is taking care of herself.

Therefore, there is no need for me to cry.

October 26, 2018

I have some characteristics that are similar to my mother even though I have not been around her all of my life.

The way she says "Oh, wow!"

I have always said that and so does my daughter. The way we say it is the exact way she says it. As I pondered on how I began to say that in the exact tone as my mother, I wondered how I could have possibly picked that up from her. Then I remembered my sister Carla used to say, "Oh, wow!" all the time.

There is a good possibility that she is the one from whom I copied it. Carla was the oldest girl and she was eight years old when our mother left. I am guessing that she would have been more likely to pick it up from our mother, and I, most likely, picked it up from her.

Our "Oh, wow!" Is probably not hereditary. It is probably environmental. I was able to see a few other characteristics that I have similar to my mother. However, since she was not around as I was growing up I wonder if I inherited from her, or if I picked them up from her before she left, or if my sister picked them up from her and I picked them up from my sister.

DIARY OF EMOTIONS: THOUGHTS AND FEELINGS
Grace LaJoy Henderson

November 1, 2018

I kind of want to go see my mother again because I want my son to meet her. I think it is important for him to meet her. At first, I thought we would bring her here and all of her grandchildren would meet her at that time. Now, I do not think she will ever come here.

The thought of moving there has occurred to me. It was only a passing thought, however. I do not actually foresee that ever happening. Besides, I do not think she would welcome that close of a relationship anyway. She has been on her own for a very long time and, actually, so have I. It would probably be uncomfortable for us both.

She has been living her life and she does not really need anyone. Sometimes, I feel like I want to take on a more active role. For example, she would say to me, "I need this." or "I want that." I would provide it, so that she would never feel like she does not have what she needs or wants.

It looks like her basic needs are already being cared for. The boarding home washes her clothes regularly, and they distribute her medication. I would love to do more things for her that she wants. However, having more things would surely cause her to stand out among the other residents at the boarding home. It could make her an even wider target for the residents to continue to steal her stuff.

DIARY OF EMOTIONS: THOUGHTS AND FEELINGS
Grace LaJoy Henderson

Sometimes, I think about the fact that there is actually another Geneva living in the same boarding home where my mother, Geneva, lives. The other Geneva actually has my mother's maiden name. So, on the day I found my mother, if I would have asked for her maiden name, the other Geneva may have come to the phone and I may have thought I had found the wrong Geneva and given up looking.

Thankfully, I asked for the correct last name and the right Geneva came to the phone. When she came to the phone, her voice did not sound the way I expected, however, I later realized it did sound a lot like the voice my father would often mock for her. He had her voice down pat. I guess she has the same voice now as she had forty-nine years ago. I just did not actually remember her voice.

I have pondered the idea of bringing my mother to live in my home with me. That, too, is nothing more than a passing thought. Since she and I do not really know each other, that would likely not be a good decision.

Sometimes, I think that if I could have a job working at home, then I could take care of her because I would be home all the time. However, she would still require a place to go every day to get the behavioral therapy she needs. Whenever I ponder this idea, I think about a mental health nurse coming into the home to assist with that. Sometimes, I feel like I could handle taking care of her long-term. Other times, I feel like I would be getting in way over my head.

Sometimes, I think about what April and Donna said about as long as she takes her medication, she is okay. Other times, I realize caring for her may be a challenge, for which I am not prepared. Hearing April say, "If she were my mother, I would have her living with me," is what gave me the idea that maybe I could be successful with taking care of her. However, April is a trained professional in the field and I am not.

This part of the diary entry is just a representation of the many times I have thought about having my mother live with me. I do not see that as ever being a real possibility. However, it is interesting for me to think about it from time to time.

DIARY OF EMOTIONS: THOUGHTS AND FEELINGS
Grace LaJoy Henderson

November 20, 2018

I am having afterthoughts about our reunion. Grayson, Terrance and myself went back to the boarding home the very next day to have dinner with our mother; and we took chicken. My brother Jerome declined the opportunity to go back. His initial intentions were to go there, see our mother, enjoy her, take a picture or two to share the wonderful memory with his son and maybe our nieces and nephews.

My intentions were different. I wanted to spend every moment that I could with her while we were there, and then try to get her to come back with us so we could take care of her and build a relationship.

I think Jerome just automatically knew what we were up against and I did not. I thought Mother would jump at the opportunity to be with us if only she knew that my father was no longer around. I had always thought she left because of how he treated her. I never would have expected that she left of her own accord and that she wanted to be gone.

DIARY OF EMOTIONS: THOUGHTS AND FEELINGS
Grace LaJoy Henderson

November 22, 2018

I called my mother today. When I told her today was my birthday, she sang the "Happy Birthday" song to me. I thought that was nice of her. She sang… "Happy birthday to you, happy birthday to you, happy birthday dear Grace, happy birthday to you."

I could picture her with a wide smile on her face.

I had never heard my own mother sing "Happy Birthday" to me in my entire life. I had assorted feelings throughout the song.

During this phone call, I finally got a chance to talk to my mother about the package I sent. She confirmed she had received it. She said she likes the yarn and knitting needles I sent. She has not begun using them for two reasons: she does not have an instruction book, and she wants more yarn so that she may knit a large men's sweater.

At her request, I had also included cod liver oil. She told me that she took it a couple of times and then somebody stole it. I felt disappointed. I am beginning to see for myself that she really cannot have anything of value at the boarding home. Thoughts of, "she should be living here with us," came to my mind. However, I know she is happy there. The thought of never sending anything there again also came to my mind.

After this phone call, I ended up sending her a couple of instruction books, so that she may get started knitting something.

DIARY OF EMOTIONS: THOUGHTS AND FEELINGS
Grace LaJoy Henderson

I did not send more yarn for a men's sweater. I wanted to know she was using the yarn I already sent before sending more.

    I felt a bit guilty for not sending the additional yarn she had asked for, but I was just not convinced that if I sent more that she would actually use it.

DIARY OF EMOTIONS: THOUGHTS AND FEELINGS
Grace LaJoy Henderson

December 1, 2018

Just thinking about my mother and wondering what I would do if her boarding home or center called to say she needs someone to care of her. This brought a couple of questions to my mind. What if our only opportunity to bring her closer to us was after she can no longer care for herself.

What would we do?

Should we jump at the opportunity to bring our mother closer to us under those circumstances?

I am not going to attempt to answer these questions right now. I may have one response today and a different response tomorrow. I believe my mother's mental illness has controlled all of her decisions. Should that make these types of questions easier to answer?

DIARY OF EMOTIONS: THOUGHTS AND FEELINGS
Grace LaJoy Henderson

January 23, 2019

I am thinking about the last conversation I had with my mother. I had not talked to her in a few weeks. Normally I would call every other week or so, but it had been around four weeks or more since I called. More time had gone by than usual. Well anyway, I called, she came to the phone, and she seemed happy to hear from me.

The first thing she said was, "I received the box you sent me."

Actually, she had already told me she received the box the last time we spoke. I had sent it before Christmas and we had already discussed it. She had already told me she liked everything I sent. I did not tell her we had already had that conversation.

We began to talk.

"Have you talked to Carla?" she asked.

I told her, "No, I have not talked to Carla. We still don't know where she is."

She inquired, "Have you talked to Terrance?"

"No. I have not."

She always asks about Carla and Terrance. My response is usually the same.

I asked, "How is your hip doing?"

"It feels uncomfortable, but it feels better since I got that shot to help with the pain. I still have to go to the doctor."

DIARY OF EMOTIONS: THOUGHTS AND FEELINGS
Grace LaJoy Henderson

I felt like if she were in Kansas City, we would have taken her to the doctor for her hip a long time ago. It seems like she is very cooperative with the services provided by the center.

This is the phone call when she reminded me Valentine's Day was coming up. I guess if you grew up with my grandmother, as she did, you are going to enjoy those special days. Grandmother always observed special occasions.

She celebrated moments that were not holidays, too. Like, when she would bring me milkshakes at bedtime. Around the winter holidays, Grandmother would put up a tree, buy presents, bake cookies, and sing holiday songs. Grandmother was just a wonderful person. I could see why my mother would look forward to special occasions.

After we talked for a bit, she told me that the office worker was indicating to her that somebody else needed to use the phone.

I said, "Okay."

She said, "Thank you for calling. I like hearing your voice."

I said, "Thank you. I will try to call sooner next time."

She said, "Okay."

She did not seem like she really cared about how long it took me to call. She seemed like she was just happy that I had called when I did.

January 23, 2019

Just reminiscing about our very first reunion visit, when I asked my mother if she wanted me to find the children she had after she left us, and she said, "Yes."

I used the information she gave me to search for them. I even located a couple of people who I thought could actually be my siblings. After an unfavorable experience, I gave up searching for my siblings, at least for now.

Besides, I am still toiling concerning my relationship with my mother. Should I take on the responsibility of bringing new long-lost family into the equation at this time?

DIARY OF EMOTIONS: THOUGHTS AND FEELINGS
Grace LaJoy Henderson

April 20, 2019

Today I was discussing a psychological theory. I was talking about how if a person is poor, and lives in a community that is not poor, that person may have more stress than if he or she lived in a place where everybody is poor.

This reminded me of my mother because she prefers to stay in the poor area where she is, even though we have offered her an opportunity to live in a community that is not poor.

When my brothers and I found her, we offered her the opportunity to come live in Kansas City with us. We showed her a beautiful place where she could live and told her how we wanted to take care of her. She did not outright reject it, but she said no to it because she likes where she is.

According to the center director, my mother is surrounded by drugs every day. According to my mother, she is surrounded by people who constantly steal from her. She is afraid to walk around in her community for fear of harm. If she does not go get her food in time, another resident will take her plate of food and eat it.

Nevertheless, that is her home and she is content to live there.

We have offered to move her to a place where she would not be surrounded by drugs, where people would not steal from her, where she would not have live in fear. She declined because she felt that what we were offering her was "luxury" and that she is not ready for anything like that right now.

She said, "I am used to where I am at. I kind of like it here."

Based on her response to our offer, I feel she may not be comfortable living in a community that was not poor.

Besides, sometimes I wonder: Would she still feel like she needs to carry her backpack around, to protect all of her belongings, even if she were in a place where nobody would steal from her?

Well anyway, we decided to let it go and not try to convince her to come away from the place where she is comfortable. If she is happy living there, then we are happy for her.

DIARY OF EMOTIONS: THOUGHTS AND FEELINGS
Grace LaJoy Henderson

April 20, 2019

I was talking to my mother today. She was asleep, they woke her up, she sounded tired, but she came to the phone. She said that her hip had been giving her more trouble than usual. She said she saw the doctor at the center and they gave her some medication that makes her tired and sleepy. I guess that was why she was sleeping so well.

I asked her if she needed anything.

She said she needed some cigarettes.

When I was there, one of the boarding home workers had told me her favorite kind of cigarettes, and they were not very expensive. I actually thought cigarettes cost a lot more than that nowadays. At that price, my brothers and I had bought her a whole case of them while we were there.

While we were on the phone, I told her I already knew her favorite cigarettes since we bought them for her when we were there. She told me those cigarettes were not actually her favorite, but that her favorites were an expensive name brand cigarette; and that was what she wanted. She said she only smoked the more affordable cigarettes because she did not have the money to buy her favorite brand.

I actually feel guilty about the idea of sending cigarettes, let alone the most expensive ones, because I do not believe they are good for her health. I did not say that to her because I did not feel like I knew her well enough, and I did not want to come off as being judgmental.

I don't know.

Should I have just said it anyway?

Nevertheless, as I was preparing to send them, I found out it was against the law to send tobacco through the mail. I decided I would just send money instead. However, there are challenges to sending money because she does not have any way of cashing a check or a money order. The only option is to risk sending cash.

I wish there was some other way to get money to her.

DIARY OF EMOTIONS: THOUGHTS AND FEELINGS
Grace LaJoy Henderson

April 28, 2019

On this day, I learned that my mother actually knows how to initiate a phone call to me. I have mixed feelings about it because she never calls me. I always initiate the phone calls to her and sometimes she does not come to the phone and does not return my calls. When she does come to the phone, she finds a reason to get off.

Today was different.

I had sent her some money, in lieu of cigarettes, and she did not receive it. She actually initiated a phone call to me, even though I had not called her first and even though the workers at her boarding home did not encourage her to make the call. She was calling because she had not received the money that I sent.

She called two times in a row but my phone was on silent and I did not get the calls. I realized she called when I saw the boarding home phone number on my list of missed calls and heard her talking on my voicemail.

She had never called me before.

I was not sure if I should be happy because she finally called me, or sad because she only called because she had not received the money.

DIARY OF EMOTIONS: THOUGHTS AND FEELINGS
Grace LaJoy Henderson

May 12, 2019

I am still feeling discouraged about the cash I sent last month never arriving, so I did not send a Mother's Day card for fear it would not reach her.

Instead, I called my mother today to tell her Happy Mother's Day, but the phone just rang and no one answered. I tried a few more times this evening, but still no answer.

May 13, 2019

I called my mother again today because I did not want her to feel like I skipped acknowledging her for Mother's Day.

The boarding home worker who answered the phone told me she was not going to come to the phone, and did not bother with going to get her.

I have not heard from her anymore since the cash I sent got lost in the mail. I have tried calling her since then, but she did not come to the phone. Therefore, after today, I may not be calling or sending anything for a while.

June 16, 2019

I called Mother today. The boarding home worker told me that she was in her room and that she was not going to come to the phone. That is the same thing the worker told me the last time I called about a month ago. The time before that, my mother chose not to come to the phone.

This is the third time in a row that I called and have not been able to speak with her. I am not sure if it is her choice or if the worker just does not feel like going to get her to come to the phone.

I feel sad about it, but it is okay.

At least I found her and I know where she is.

DIARY OF EMOTIONS: THOUGHTS AND FEELINGS
Grace LaJoy Henderson

August 6, 2019

I am still toiling about whether or not it is best, for my mother, if I continue to initiate communication with her. Nevertheless, I went on and sent her a care package. I called to let her know the package should have arrived, and spoke to her only briefly.

She said she would ask about it.

I called the next day to ensure she received it.

When I called this time, I told the boarding home worker I do not need to speak to her. I just wanted to confirm she received the package.

The worker jokingly said, "She would just think of a reason to get off the phone anyway."

I said, "Yeah."

We both laughed about it.

In reality, that truth was very hurtful for me.

The worker went and asked her, then came back to the phone to confirm that my mother had received it.

I said, "thank you," and we ended the call.

DIARY OF EMOTIONS: THOUGHTS AND FEELINGS
Grace LaJoy Henderson

September 15, 2019

The last time I called the boarding home was when I called to confirm with my mother that she received the care package. I do not feel I should call her anymore.

I will continue to acknowledge her for special occasions. However, I think it is best for me, and for her, if I discontinue the phone calls.

She has been on her own for so many years and I think she is happy that way. Her actions have shown me four things:

That she appreciates our interest.

That she likes receiving gifts and money, mostly money.

That she prefers to be to herself.

That maybe she would be more content without the phone calls.

When she abandoned me when I was only two years old, I said to my grandmother, "Well if she don't want me, I don't want her *needer*." Today I say, "Well, if she don't want to talk to me, I don't want to talk to her *needer*." Overall, if she prefers to be to herself, then I will respect that.

I will always be grateful that I found her and happy that I know where she is.

DIARY OF EMOTIONS: THOUGHTS AND FEELINGS
Grace LaJoy Henderson

September 22, 2019

I sent my mother a small package just to acknowledge her. I did not call her to let her know to look out for it the way I normally would. I just sent it and tried not worry about it. I really wanted to know if it was placed in her hands.

It is hard to send things without calling because I like to let her know to expect it. I also like to confirm she received it.

But, whenever I call, I have to contend with her either not coming to the phone, not calling me back, or acting like she needs to get off the phone; although, I am always more than willing to let her go as soon as I discuss the package I sent.

Calling her is uncomfortable because I feel like she would be content without me calling her. I know she likes receiving things, but there are challenges to me sending packages.

Besides the risk of it getting lost in the mail, it causes her to have to carry even more items around in her already heavy backpack. If she stores it in her bedroom, it will be stolen.

Therefore, I have every reason to stop calling and to stop sending things.

September 24, 2019

I ended up calling my mother this evening. I called to let her know the small package should have been delivered to her by now and to see if she had received it.

Here is how the call went:

The boarding home worker called her to the phone and she actually came! As she was picking up the phone to begin talking to me, I heard the boarding home worker say, "You only have two minutes, other people need to use the phone. This is a business phone."

I know from my own personal experience with the boarding home, that their phone hardly ever rings.

Was there really someone else who wanted to use the phone?

Was the worker serious about the phone being only for business, and not for personal calls?

Was the worker helping Geneva to be able to make a clean exit from our phone call?

Well, whatever the case, my mother sounded vibrant and happy to hear from me. I told her I heard what the boarding home worker said, so I would not keep her on the phone for a long time. I told her I sent her a package and just wanted to see if she had received it.

She seemed very interested and asked me to confirm the address I mailed it to. She said she had not received it, but she would be sure to check on it the next day.

I told her it would be nice if she could call me the next day to let me know, but that she did not have to.

She began asking questions about how my day was going and what I had been doing. I answered, then, in turn, I asked her how she had been doing. She sounded like she was really enjoying me and that she was happy I called.

I was feeling confused because of what I heard the boarding home worker say. I answered her questions very briefly and tried not to engage her in too much more conversation.

During this call, my mother said, "You know that last package you sent me?"

I said, "Yes."

She said, "My roommate stole it!"

I said, "That is horrible!" I saw it as a care package gone down the drain, but I could not blame anybody but myself. I knew the type of environment she lived in when I sent it.

This became the deciding factor that I absolutely will not be sending my mother any more packages.

She did not call the next day to let me know if she received the current package, so I did not call her either.

I figured either she got it or she didn't.

IN CLOSING...

As far as calling and sending things are concerned: I have resolved to simply sending a small card with a very, very small amount of cash inside, only on special occasions. I will refrain from calling to confirm if she has received it.

If the amount I send is small enough, then I will not need to worry myself about whether she received it.

If I stop sending packages, then I can stop worrying about them getting lost in the mail, or being stolen by her roommates, and I will not need to call to confirm whether she received the things.

If she ever wants to talk to me, she can call because she has my phone number.

So many times, people see reunions like ours and assume things were happily ever after. They never find out what *really* happened after the reunion. The questions, the challenges, the toiling. In spite of all of that, I would find my mother again, and again, and again.

These emotions, thoughts and feelings I have experienced are nothing compared to actually finding my mother.

DIARY OF EMOTIONS: THOUGHTS AND FEELINGS
Grace LaJoy Henderson

Discussion Questions

1. Do you think Grace should keep calling and sending things to her mother? Why or why not?
2. Do you believe Grace has forgiven her mother for leaving her when she was two years old? Why or why not?
3. How does a mother just abandon her children and not want to be with them when they find her? Discuss your thoughts about this.
4. Do you think Mother will feel sad if Grace never calls again, even though she has Grace's phone number but never calls her? Discuss your response.
5. Do you think Grace would have had a happier life if her mentally ill mother would have never abandoned her?
6. Grace feels like her mother does not really want, or need, her in her life? Discuss your thoughts about this.
7. Grace's father expected her mother to do all the things he expected from a wife, even though she had a mental illness. What do you think about his expectations? Discuss your response.
8. What if Grace's only opportunity to bring her mother to live closer, was after her mother could no longer care for herself? Do you feel Grace should jump at the opportunity to bring her mother closer under those circumstances?

9. What are your thoughts about Grace's decision not to search for her other siblings at this time?

10. Grace felt guilty about sending her mother the cigarettes she asked for, because she believed they are not good for her health. She did not say that to her mother because she felt like she did not know her mother well enough and she did not want to come off as being judgmental. Should she have just said it anyway? Why or Why not?

DIARY OF EMOTIONS: THOUGHTS AND FEELINGS
Grace LaJoy Henderson

Questions Teachers Can Ask
Critical Thinking/In-depth Comprehension/Writing Skills/Technology Skills

1. What is the main idea or learning experience of the book?
2. Write your thoughts or feelings about the story.
3. Summarize your favorite part of the book and tell why this was your favorite part.
4. Write about an experience in your personal life and tell how it is similar to this story.
5. Write a new summary for the book.
6. To whom would you recommend this book? Why?
7. How can the information in the story be useful in your life or future?
8. Research a famous or infamous person on the computer who was abandoned by their mother, and write a report about that person's life.
9. Research a famous or infamous person on the computer who suffered from a mental illness, and write a report about that person's life.
10. Find a book in the library written by an author who has published their personal diary, and discuss how that book is different from this one.

DIARY OF EMOTIONS: THOUGHTS AND FEELINGS
Grace LaJoy Henderson

Further Discussion Points

Diary of Emotions indicated some of the Effects this has had on the author. Below are some excerpts, from the book, that you may use for additional discussion about mental health.

Effects on the author

Motherly instincts took author by surprise. After being away from Geneva for so many years, the author felt surprised when Geneva showed motherly instincts. Read and discuss the excerpts below.

However, one time we were talking on the phone and I told her I was not feeling well. She immediately started giving me pointers about how to take care of myself, you know, like a mother would do. I just said, "Yeah," as if to tell her, "I already know how to take care of myself." I felt surprised that her motherly instinct actually stepped up in that moment. My first instinct was to feel like I did not need a mother. In a way, I felt honored that she showed that she cared. In another way, it felt unusual for her to act "motherly" towards me after being away for my entire life. **Page 54-55**

I called my mother today. When I told her today was my birthday, she sang the "Happy Birthday" song to me. I thought that was nice of her. She sang... "Happy birthday to you, happy birthday to you, happy birthday dear Grace, happy birthday to you." I could picture her with a wide smile on her face. I had never heard my own mother sing "Happy Birthday" to me in my entire life. I had assorted feelings throughout the song. **Page 83**

DIARY OF EMOTIONS: THOUGHTS AND FEELINGS
Grace LaJoy Henderson

Feeling unwanted by her mother. While the author feels grateful for finding her mother, there are some things in her story that indicate she may, at times, feel unwanted by her mother. Read and discuss the excerpt below.

Still, I asked myself, "Is her hip really hurting that badly, or is this a sign that she still does not want me after all of these years?" **Page 52**

I would hate for her to experience the same rejection from me that she experienced from my father. However, I am afraid I may approach another point in my life where I will have to say, "Well, if she don't want me, I don't want her needer." **Page 55**

I always initiate the phone calls to her and sometimes she does not come to the phone and does not return my phone call. When she does come to the phone, she finds a reason to get off. **Page 93**

These *Further Discussion Points* are only a few things that stood out for the author from her own story. Did you see any additional Effects on the author as you read the book? If so, please free to discuss them.

DIARY OF EMOTIONS: THOUGHTS AND FEELINGS
Grace LaJoy Henderson

FINDING MOTHER SERIES

A Gifted Child in Foster Care:
A Story Resilience – REVISED EDITION
In this book, Dr. Grace LaJoy shares her life story of being deserted by her mother, living in foster care, and ending up in a gifted and talented class while still in foster care. She recalls her life story before, during and after foster care. The *Finding Mother Series* was written as a sequel to this book.

Finding Mother After Five Decades:
A Story of Hope
Grace LaJoy's determination pays off when she finally finds her mother who abandoned her at age two. Discover the specific details about her intriguing journey in **Finding Mother after Five Decades,** BOOK 1 of the *Finding Mother Series.*

Reuniting with Mother:
A Story of Tenacity
What happens when Grace LaJoy and her siblings come face-to-face with their estranged mother after 49 years? How does she receive them? Find out in **Reuniting with Mother,** BOOK 2 of the *Finding Mother Series.*

DIARY OF EMOTIONS: THOUGHTS AND FEELINGS
Grace LaJoy Henderson

After the Reunion:
A Story of Acceptance
After a very emotional reunion, Grace LaJoy has two concerns to address with her long-lost mother. What are her concerns? Does she get the answers she needs from her mother? Find out in **After the Reunion,** BOOK 3 of the *Finding Mother Series.*

Diary of Emotion:
Thoughts and Feelings
After reuniting with her mother after 49 years, Grace LaJoy toils with an array of thoughts and feeling. She reveals them all in **Diary of Emotions,** BOOK 4 of the *Finding Mother Series.*

Available in softcover and Kindle eBook
Collect them all at Amazon.com
Ask for the series in
bookstores and libraries
www.gracelajoy.com

DIARY OF EMOTIONS: THOUGHTS AND FEELINGS
Grace LaJoy Henderson

PRAISES FOR THE FINDING MOTHER SERIES

Grace LaJoy Henderson's *Finding Mother Series* is a revelation. It is a gift to discover an author who can write so honestly—and with such vulnerability—about the joy and pain of reuniting with a parent after a 49-year separation. Henderson never glosses over the frightening or disappointing parts of her story. But her compassionate, unwavering voice, as she uncovers the long arc of her mother's life, is itself a triumph. ~**Whitney Terrell, Associate Professor of English, University of Missouri-Kansas City**

"The author's emotional honesty and the balancing of positive and negative emotions is what makes this series work." ~**Phoebe Shanahan, MA in English Literature**

"The Finding Mother Series will inspire readers to *feel* their feelings. It stirs people in similar situations to be at peace, but at the same time seek growth, in the midst of their circumstances." **Arica Miller, LMSW, School Social Worker**

"The *Finding Mother Series* displays a perfect example of how one triggering event can cause conflicting emotions. Throughout the series, the author experienced hope *and* despair, excitement *and* apprehension. Two, totally opposite emotions both at the same time. However, both were completely justified! This range and transition of emotions is what drives the entire *series*. Secondary students will absolutely benefit from reading this collection of books." ~**Jacob Kelow, M.S.Ed., Secondary School Counselor, Kansas City Public Schools**

PRAISES continued →

DIARY OF EMOTIONS: THOUGHTS AND FEELINGS
Grace LaJoy Henderson

"The *Finding Mother Series* is written in a very powerful, real and authentic voice style. The author's honesty shines through her writing. Although the author's sadness throughout the story is quite palpable, her attitude towards her mentally ill mother is full of grace and understanding despite the fact that she had abandoned her. This is a clear and honest work." **~Fay Collins, Writer-Editor**

"The *Finding Mother Series* is a beautiful sequence of books. The author's reunion with her mother is very well documented." **~Phyllis Harris, Former Missouri State Director, Parent Information Resource Center**

"The author shares her personal story in an authentic way. Easy reading. Flows well." **~Ila Barrett, Behavioral Therapist, Jacksonville, FL**

"The Finding Mother Series is an inspiration to all who have faced abandonment by a parent. Grace LaJoy's truth validates her determination never to extinguish the fire, which burned in her soul to find her mother." **~ Dr. Gwendolyn Squires, Former School Principal, Kansas City Public Schools**

"Reading this series may help others who long to be reunited with their parents." **~Dr. Mary E. McConnell, Educator, University of Missouri-Kansas City**

"The Finding Mother Series will touch many people who are in this same situation, but who may not have the forgiveness in their hearts that the author and her siblings have. It is going to touch lives in more ways than you can imagine." **~Jean Smith, Dallas, TX**

"I strongly believe that this series will heal a lot of broken hearts and act as a source of encourage, advice, guidance and counsel for people in such scenarios; both children and adults." **~Ken J.**

About the Author

Dr. Grace LaJoy Henderson is the author of over thirty books. Her foster care story, *A Gifted Child in Foster Care: A Story of Resilience, Classroom Set* and her children's book series, *The Gracie Series*, are currently being used in public and charter schools.

Pearson Higher Education published two chapters from her foster care story in a college textbook.

She has earned a Doctorate in Christian Counseling, a Master's of Education in Guidance and Counseling, and a Master of Arts in Curriculum and Instruction. She has also earned a Bachelor's degree in Social Psychology.

Dr. Henderson managed a contract with the Missouri Children's Division, in which she provided court ordered mentoring for foster youth, supervised parent-child visits and parent education. She has served as psychology and college success instructor as well as academic coach. Outside of higher education, she is a keynote speaker, workshop leader and guest author at schools, libraries and other organizations. Newspapers, radio and television has featured her publications and her story.

DIARY OF EMOTIONS: THOUGHTS AND FEELINGS
Grace LaJoy Henderson

www.ingramcontent.com/pod-product-compliance
Lightning Source LLC
Chambersburg PA
CBHW052101070526
44584CB00017B/2280